GETTING TO KNOW YOU
Sally Featherstone
and Clare Beswick
Simple games
to play with
your baby

INTRODUCTION

We all know how important it is for new mums and dads to play with their babies from the earliest days but there are times when even the best parents need a bit of extra help to inspire and encourage them. *Getting to know you* does exactly that! It provides simple games that you can play with even the youngest baby with the minimum of equipment and nothing more than a little bit of your time and energy. Experts in baby development have proved that these baby games help with brain development as well as with more visible skills such as hand-eye coordination and mobility.

On every page of this book you will find a simple but effective game that you and your baby can enjoy together. Each game is accompanied by a 'Tiny tips' panel that provides additional advice on how to get the most out of the activity and a 'Did you know?' feature that gives you background information on how your baby is developing and learning.

Spending time with your baby and showing how much you love them is one of the most important things you can do to help your baby grow and develop. This book aims to inspire you at the beginning of your fascinating learning journey together!

Tiny tips

- Give yourself plenty of time to enjoy this song with your baby.
- Spending time with your baby will really help them feel happy, secure and settled.

HELLO

Singing hello, stroking cheeks

1. Hold your baby close so that you can gaze into each other's faces.

2. Tickle your baby's cheek gently and sing 'Hello *name*, hello *name*, hello, hello, hello.'

3. Put a teddy in your baby's arms, hug the two of them together and sing 'Hello *name*, hello *name*, hello, hello, hello.'

4. Put the teddy down, and sing 'Hello' to your baby again.

5. Take your time, stroking your baby's cheek and giving them plenty of time to focus on your face.

Another idea: When your baby is lying down, gently rub their hands in yours, as you sing the song again.

Did you know?

Newborn babies naturally respond to music. Even the tiniest of babies can be soothed with familiar songs and tunes.

HUG BUG I LOVE YOU

Blowing kisses, fingers, nose and toes

1. Hold your baby really close. Trail your fingers slowly and gently over their hands. Whisper to your baby 'Hug bug, I love you,' and kiss their hands.

2. Gently rub their feet and toes as you whisper 'Hug bug, I love you,' and gently kiss their toes.

3. Stroke their face gently, first along their cheeks, then across the temples and down the sides of their face, down to their chin, and then slowly down the bridge of their nose. Gaze lovingly at your baby and whisper 'Hug bug, I love you' and gently kiss the end of their nose.

Another idea: Rest your baby gently on your chest, supporting their head. Stroke their back rhythmically as you whisper 'Hug bug, I love you'. Finish with a tiny kiss on the side of their head.

Tiny tips

- Repeat the game a few times. Your baby will soon learn to anticipate a kiss!
- When they know the game, pause for just a moment and see if they look at you to 'ask' for that kiss!

Did you know?

Babies need to know you love them. Frequent close contact is very important for their growth and well being.

Tiny tips

• Bring your baby's hand up to your face so they can feel your skin and hair. Blow gently on their fingertips.

• Give your baby plenty of time to watch and copy your expressions.

LOOK AT ME, LOOK AT YOU

Imitating expressions

1. Sit with your knees raised to form a comfy backrest and head support for your baby. Prop up your baby facing you. Rest your arms on a cushion if you need to.

2. Make sure your face is near enough for your baby to see you clearly – tiny babies focus best at between 20 and 30cm, around 8 to 12 inches.

3. Talk gently to your baby, sometimes opening your mouth wide or sticking your tongue out a bit. Watch to see if your baby copies you.

4. Sing to your baby as you play, doing actions with your mouth and tongue. Copy any actions they make.

Another idea: Move gently from side to side, talking all the time. Move slowly so that they can follow your face with their gaze.

Did you know?

From three hours old, babies will start to copy your expressions. Make these faces slowly and wait patiently for their response.

Tiny tips

- Look out for dappled sunlight and shade. Watch your baby's fascination with shafts of sunlight or leaves shimmering on trees.
- Take time to look at coloured lights and shiny objects.

LIGHT AND SHADE

Contrasts of light

1. Show your baby brightly coloured or reflective objects, such as a baby mirror, one at a time. Give them plenty of time to look.

2. Help them to feel the objects. Shake them for your baby.

3. Change the light in the room, perhaps by sitting next to a blind or curtain, or adjusting a dimmer switch. Show your baby the objects again and encourage them to look at and feel them.

Another idea: Put together a small basket of reflective toys or everyday objects for you and your baby to explore together.

Did you know?

Contrasts in colour, light and pattern fascinate babies. They will watch and follow the edges of shapes and patterns very closely.

Did you know?

Your baby will begin to recognise your face from the very first day! From about three days they will know you.

MAKE A FACE

Looking at black and white face patterns

1. Make the face by drawing a clear, simple mouth, eyes and a nose on the card. Make the mouth smiling. Don't add too many features – at this age babies respond best to simple images with lots of contrast. Add a stick if you have one.

2. Sit your baby somewhere comfortable – in a baby chair, a bean bag or well propped up with cushions. Take special care that their head is well supported.

3. Hold the face where your baby can see it (not too close).

4. Talk to them to attract their attention. Watch how they look at the face. Watch for looking, kicking, arm waving.

Another idea: Make some more faces. Use different colours and different expressions. Watch what your baby does as you change from one face to another. Don't go on too long!

Tiny tips

• Young babies focus best on faces and objects held at about 22cm from their eyes. This is about the distance from your elbow to your wrist.

Tiny tips

- Pointing may be a new movement for your baby, but it is an important step in developing muscle control.
- Take your time. Babies need time to explore new things with their eyes before touching or holding.

FEELY STUFF

First sensory play

1. Hold your baby in your arms and take them for a little 'feeling' walk around your home or outside.

2. Stop and look at things as you go – a flower or leaf, the pattern on the wallpaper, a reflection in a mirror, an ornament, or a family photo.

3. As you stop and look, talk about the object you are looking at. Reach out and touch it, tell your baby what it is called, and what it feels like.

4. If your baby waves their hands let them feel the object too. They won't be able to make very accurate contact, so watch out for valuable or fragile things!

Another idea: Find some fabrics with contrasting stripes or black and white designs.

Did you know?

Touching surfaces and textures will stimulate your baby's skin and encourage them to move their hands, arms and legs.

LET'S DANCE

Hugging and dancing

1. Hold your baby in your arms. Hold them close, and support their head. Make sure you can see their face and they can see yours.

2. Start to move gently to the music, keeping the beat and dancing round the room. Gentle rocking and swaying will stimulate your baby's brain cells.

3. Sing or hum as you move. It doesn't matter if you don't know the words, just keep humming and moving, or make up some silly, baby words.

Another idea: Sing to your baby as you feed them or change them. Don't be embarrassed about singing nonsense words and baby talk. Just keep up the gentle noises. Use the radio or a CD to help you. Pop and classical music both work!

Tiny tips

• Start with songs you like and know well. Your baby may have heard these in the womb, and they will still recognise them. Watch for kicks, waves and smiles!

Did you know?

Rhythm, movement and music are all important for your baby's brain. Rocking, dancing and singing will help their brain to grow.

BLACK AND WHITE
Reaching for patterns

1. Make a simple mobile to hang above your baby's cot or changing mat, or tie things to a baby gym.

2. Cut some circles from card.

3. Draw black patterns on the circles – spots, spirals, circles, faces and wiggly lines. Thick lines will make a good contrast.

4. Make holes in the circles and hang them from a hoop or baby gym with ribbon or string (or you could hang them from the ceiling, or from a coat hanger).

5. Put your baby on a blanket or in a chair, where they can see and reach to touch the hanging circles.

Another idea: Stick some tiny bells to the back of some of the circles.

Tiny tips

• Make sure the cards are within 30cm of your baby's eyes, but not so close that they get their hands tangled in the strings!

• Sit and talk to them while they play.

Did you know?

Simple mobiles will encourage your baby to begin to reach for things and soon to grab and hold them.

SHARE A SMILE

Eye contact and looking at faces

1. Hold your baby close, at your eye level, so that you can see their face and feel if their body is tense or relaxed.

2. Walk slowly about the room, rocking and swaying gently from side to side. Stop for a moment, smile at your baby and rub noses. Wait to see how they respond and then set off again.

3. Repeat a couple of times, each time gazing intently at your baby, showing them how much you love them, and rubbing noses.

Another idea: Look out for mobiles, toys and books with faces and face patterns.

Tiny tips

• Babies love to look at faces, particularly the faces of people they love.

• Your baby's first smile will be in response to your face smiling at them.

Did you know?

Tiny babies love looking at faces. At first they look at your outline. They can see edges of shapes more easily because of the clear line of contrast.

Tiny tips

- Babies need to touch things and put them in their mouths. Nerves in their mouths hands and fingers work with their eyes to help them learn about the world.
- Give your baby time and gently guide their hands to reach, touch and hold things.

TICKLE, TICKLE

A gentle tickling game

1. Lay your baby down on a blanket. Gently hold their hand or put your hand on their tummy for reassurance.

2. Gently tickle the palm of your baby's hand with a feather or fur fabric. Watch to see how they let you know if they like it, if they want more or if it feels strange to them.

3. Talk to your baby and share their delight in the feeling of the feather and fur against their skin.

Another idea: Sing 'Round and round the garden like a teddy bear, one step, two steps, tickle you under there'. Take the feather and make tiny circles on the palm of their hand, and then gently touch them on the arm with the feather, on 'one step, two steps', then finally on the cheek.

Did you know?

You are your baby's favourite plaything, and your love, voice and time are what he or she wants and needs.

PAT IT

Patting and kicking

1. Put your baby on a blanket or in a chair.

2. Put a glove or sock on your hand and wave it slowly at your baby. Remember to keep it near enough for them to focus, but not too near.

3. Now put the glove or sock hand near enough for the baby to reach and pat. If they can't do it themselves, help them gently to pat. Sing 'Pat a cake' as you pat.

4. If your baby is ready for more, hold the sock or glove hand where they can kick it with bare feet or socks on.

Another idea: Play the patting and kicking game with a toy with a bell or something else that makes a noise. Try with other textures – a soft balloon, a teddy, a saucepan lid or a book.

Did you know?

Kicking, patting and waving are all good practice for standing, walking, running and holding.

Tiny tips

- Patting and kicking, alone or with your assistance, will help your baby to explore more textures and objects.
- Kicking and feeling with bare feet helps develop foot and toe muscles.

Tiny tips

- Sing and talk to your baby all the time. Tell them what you are doing.
- Take your baby with you from room to room and chat to them even when you are busy doing other things.

SPLISH, SPLASH

Bath time songs

1. When your baby is resting happily in the bath, support them with one hand, and with your free hand, gently splash a few drops of water from the sponge or cloth onto their toes.

2. As you do this, sing 'Splish, splash, splosh, *name* needs a wash, splish, splash, splosh'.

3. Next, gently rub a warm flannel through their fingers, and say, 'Fingers next'. Sing again, 'Splish, splash, splosh, *name* needs a wash'.

4. Continue, dripping water on their fingers, toes and, if your baby is happy with the game, on their tummy.

Another idea: Soak the sponge and help your baby to pat it. Try different sorts of sponges for some gentle bath time fun.

Did you know?

Babies are soothed and comforted by a calm, lower pitched voice. Use different voices as you chat and sing to your baby.

TUM TUM

Tapping rhythms on their tummy

1. Take your baby's outer layer off, and lay them down in their vest and nappy.

2. Using your child's first and family name, sing to a steady beat, for example:

'Sam Smith, Sam Smith,
I love you, I love you,
Tickle on the tum tum,
Tickle on the tum tum,
I love you, I love you.'

3. With each word, tap gently on your baby's tummy. Sit where they can see you smiling at them and so they can easily look into your eyes.

Another idea: Try changing your voice to a whisper or a croak.

Tiny tips

- This is a great game for nappy time or when you are getting them dressed.
- Don't make these sessions too long, or your baby may become over-stimulated and tired.

Did you know?

Changing time and bedtime are ideal times for a bit of fun and some first rhythms! Rhythm helps speech and memory.

RADIO GOO GOO

Familiar voices

Did you know?

Babies know their mother's voice when they are born because they have heard it from the womb. If fathers talk to their babies in the womb, they will be recognised too!

1. Babies are fascinated by the sounds other babies make and will be just as fascinated by a recording of their own voice, even though they won't know who it is!

2. As soon as your baby starts to babble or gurgle, use your mobile phone, an answering machine or a tape recorder to record the sounds they make.

3. Play these back to your baby as you sit together, and watch to see their reactions.

4. Talk about what you are hearing, saying 'Who is that? Is that a baby?'

Another idea: Get your partner and other family members to record their voices. Play these to your baby as you sit together and talk about the people you are hearing.

Tiny tips

- Don't record your baby when they are distressed, it will distress them again to hear the crying.

Tiny tips

• Try gently tying a ribbon to a toy suspended above the baby's cot. Tie the other end to their ankle, so they can make the toy move. *Never leave them alone with the game!*

LOOK AND GRAB

Rattles and songs

1. Your baby can be lying down or in a chair for this game.

2. Hold the rattle where your baby can see it. Shake the rattle gently and slowly, so your baby can follow the sound.

3. Now sing to the tune of Frère Jacques:

'Here's a rattle, here's a rattle,
Can you see? Can you see?
Can you reach and touch it?
Can you reach and touch it?
Have a go! Have a go!'

Hold the rattle near enough to be grabbed. You may need to help your baby by holding their hand in yours.

Another idea: Put the rattle on your baby's ankle, while they are lying down. This will encourage them to kick.

Did you know?

By three months, babies can see more detail. They become interested in looking around and will start to pat or swipe at objects.

UP AND DOWN

Lifting high and calling

1. Hold your baby securely in your arms.

2. Now gently lift them into the air, saying 'Here we go up, up, up'. Lift slowly, looking into their eyes and smiling as you sing.

3. Now gently bring the baby down again, saying 'Here we go down, down, down' as the baby comes down to your lap again.

4. Do it again if they are enjoying it. Stop if they seem anxious or insecure. Some babies love this game, others take a long time to get used to the feeling!

Another idea: Sit your baby in your lap, facing away from you. Play 'Here we go up, up, up' with a teddy, doll or soft toy in front of you both.

Tiny tips

- Make this game short and fun or your baby may become over-stimulated and tired.
- Rock your baby gently as you sit together. Rocking is a very soothing movement.

Did you know?

Rocking, lifting, swinging are all movements that stimulate your baby to focus their eyes, move, and enjoy your company.

TINY STROKES

Baby massage

Did you know?

Babies who are stroked and cuddled a lot develop more quickly. Gently stroking their skin stimulates babies' brains to grow.

1. This is a good way of making contact with your baby after a bath, when they are warm and relaxed. Before you dress your baby, put them on their back on a warm blanket or fluffy towel on the floor or a changing mat in a quiet place.

2. Make sure your hands are warm. Pour a few drops of oil on the palm of your hand, spread it over both hands and gently massage your baby's legs, stroking away from the body towards their feet.

3. Now stroke their arms and hands, gently opening their arms from their body.

4. Talk gently or even sing or hum as you massage their arms and body too, finishing with a gentle rub of their tummy before wrapping them in the towel or blanket for a cuddle.

Another idea: You can massage a newborn baby through their clothes without using oils. Keep the room warm and free from draughts during these sessions. Use a table or other safe surface if it is more comfortable for you.

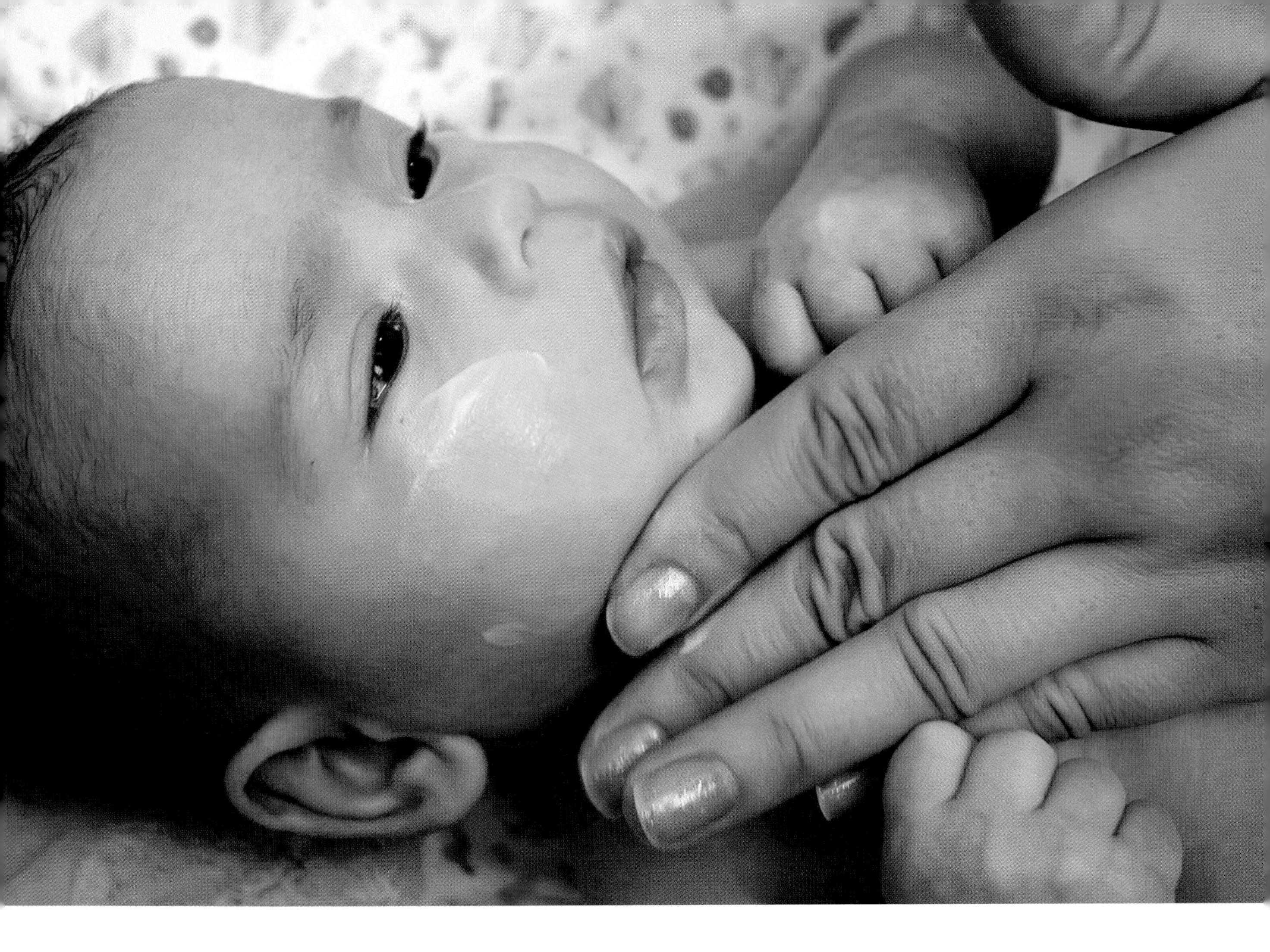

Tiny tips

• Look on the Internet for baby oils – for babies under three months old, use an organic sunflower or grapeseed oil. Over three months you can start using aromatherapy oils especially designed for babies.

• Play some quiet music or a relaxation tape on a CD player as you massage your baby.

Tiny tips

• You could start playing this game using a very thin piece of fabric such as a chiffon scarf, so your baby can still see you through it.

PEEP BO!

A first hiding game

1. This is a good game to play when your baby is in a baby chair or propped safely on some soft cushions.

2. Use a small scarf, a cot sheet or a small towel – any small piece of fabric.

3. Say your baby's name to get their attention, and then cover your own head with the fabric.

4. Slowly pull the cloth off your head to show your face – make sure you are smiling!

5. Gently say 'Boo' as your baby sees you again. Play again if they seem interested.

Another idea: If your baby loses interest, stop, and play again another day. It sometimes takes babies several times to get the hang of a new game!

Did you know?

Babies take some time to realise that when objects or people disappear, they still exist. This is why babies often get distressed when they can't see you – they think you have gone forever!

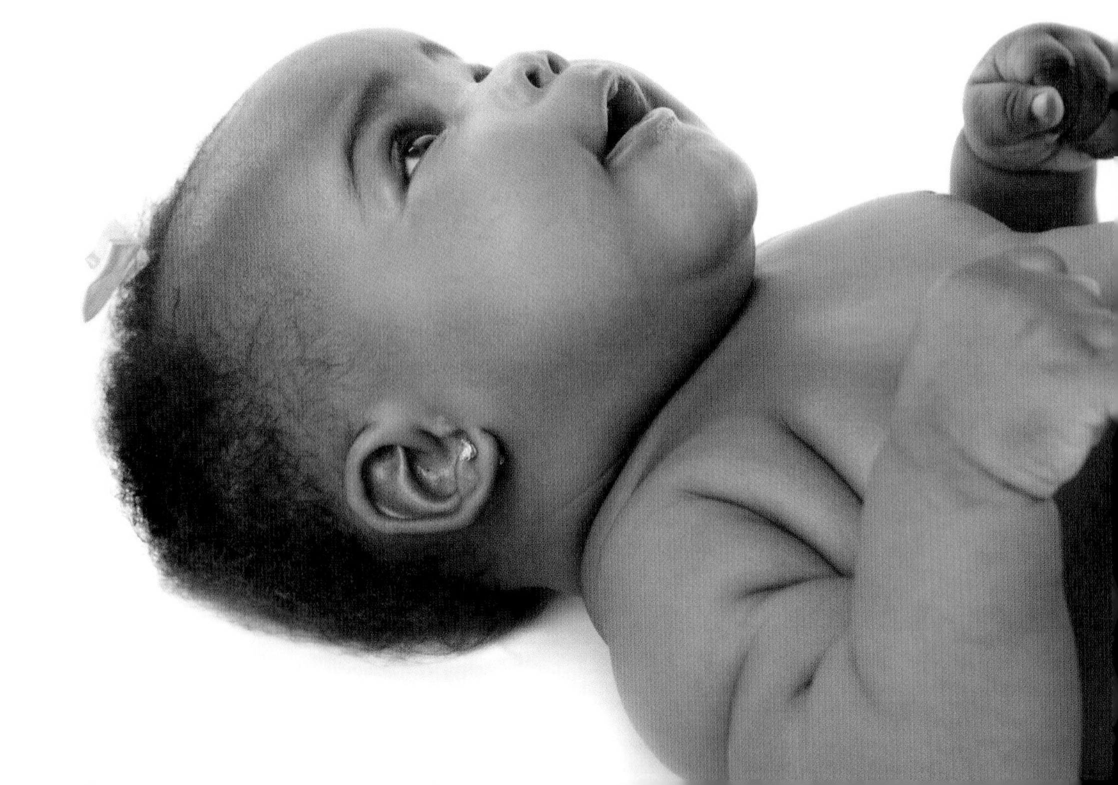

Tiny tips

- This is a good game for changing or feeding time.
- Use some of your baby's sounds, gurgles and babble by repeating it back to them. This is the start of taking turns in talking.

COPY CAT

Echoing sounds and movements

1. Sit with your baby in your lap, so your faces are level. Keep your face near so they can focus.

2. Call your baby's name or talk to them to get their attention. Use exaggerated expressions and a lively voice to maintain their interest.

3. Now look at your baby. Copy any expressions or sounds they make. If they just watch, then make a sound yourself, and leave a pause for them to reply.

4. Be patient, small babies have to work hard at copying you – their muscles are immature. Praise any response!

Another idea: Use a simple sound maker, such as a rattle or bell to stimulate or echo any sound your baby makes.

Did you know?

These copying and answering games are the first conversations you have with your baby. Taking turns is a communication skill.

LOOK OUT

What's outside the window?

1. Carry your baby in your arms or sit them in your lap so they can see outside. You can stand or sit at a window or on a doorstep, where you can see the world. Make sure the sun is not in their eyes!

2. Talk gently about the things you can see. Remember your baby will only be able to see things near at hand.

4. If the weather is suitable, open the window or door, so you can feel the fresh air, warm sunshine or breeze on your skin.

Another idea: Go for a little walk around your garden or local park, talking about what you can see. Stop to look at flowers, trees and birds.

Tiny tips

- Make sure your baby is well wrapped up, even for little walks.
- Remember that your baby can't follow moving objects easily, so focus on things that stay still.

Did you know?

This little activity helps babies to begin to look out at the wide world. Being outside is very calming and soothing for both your baby and you. Blue and green are 'feel good' colours.

Tiny tips

• Sit where the light falls on the book, so your baby can see it clearly.

• Babies respond to clear outlines and plenty of contrast, so choose books with this in mind.

ONCE UPON A TIME

Sharing books and stories

1. Your baby may not be able to understand the pictures or the words at first, but storytelling and book sharing are very important to babies. Every day (and several times a day if possible) choose a book to read with your baby.

2. Sit somewhere comfortable and warm for your stories. This could be first thing in the morning in bed, in a comfortable chair or on a sofa, on a floor cushion on, or even in the garden.

3. Hold the book where your baby can see it as you turn the pages. Lots of baby books just have one word on the page, or even no words at all. Talk about the pictures and what is happening in the book.

4. Watch how your baby responds to different books. They will soon recognise their favourites. If your baby is enjoying the book, choose another one.

Another idea: Babies soon develop favourites, and love pictures of other babies, familiar objects and animals.

Did you know?

Just reading stories to your baby will help them to learn to read - the research says so!

PAT A CAKE

A simple pat mat

1. For this game you need a plastic 'zip-lock' bag.

2. Put a small amount of water in the zip-lock bag, and add an item such as a plastic clothes peg, a baby spoon, a little plastic toy, a teething ring, and a hair 'scrunchy'.

3. Zip the bag up, squeezing out as much air as you can.

4. Now hold the bag (called a pat mat) where your baby can reach out and feel it.

5. Talk about the pat mat, hold it up to the light, and explore the contents together.

Another idea: Add some food colouring to the water in the bag.

Tiny tips

• As your baby gets older, they will love playing with these pat mats.

• Make sure they are firmly closed or tape over the end with duct tape.

• Never leave your baby alone with plastic bags of any sort.

Did you know?

Scrunching, squeezing and poking are all good for hand and finger muscles, and for making the brain work harder.

Published 2010 by A&C Black Publishers Limited
36 Soho Square, London W1D 3QY
www.acblack.com

ISBN 9781408129869

A CIP record for this publication is available from the British Library.

Printed in Spain by Grafos S.A.

This book is produced using paper that is made from wood grown in managed, sustainable forests. It is natural, renewable and recyclable. The logging and manufacturing processes conform to the environmental regulations of the country of origin.